Sex, Love, & Romance

SEX, LOVE, AND ROMANCE
Poetry from her and his point of view

Her: LaKeah Shannelle
Him: Jeff Ellis

Published by:
Hydra Productions Online LLC

Cover art by:
If someone else did your cover, please put that information here.

Jeff Ellis & LaKeah Shannelle

Title © 2021 Jeff Ellis & Lakeah Shanelle

All rights reserved under the International and Pan-American Copyright Conventions. No part of this book may be reproduced or transmitted in any form or by any means, electronic or mechanical, including photocopying, recording, or by any information storage and retrieval system, without permission in writing from the publisher.
This is a work of fiction. Names, places, characters and incidents are either the product of the author's imagination or are used fictitiously, and any resemblance to any actual persons, living or dead, organizations, events or locales is entirely coincidental.
Warning: the unauthorized reproduction or distribution of this copyrighted work is illegal. Criminal copyright infringement, including infringement without monetary gain, is investigated by the FBI and is punishable by up to 5 years in prison and a fine of $250,000.

Dedication
You can put a couple of short lines in dedication here. Please make sure it is centered and italicized. You may also replace this with a one-page Acknowledgements, also italicized, but it will not be centered or indented.

Jeff Ellis & LaKeah Shannelle

LaKeah's Thoughts

WHO KNEW?

Who knew?
You said you didn't,
Our lips touched and
The electricity
Could light up a field.
Your hand that slid down
To my hip
Left a fire in its wake.
My softness held your hardness Tightly, erotically,
My nectar nourished youR thirst, lovingly.

Who knew? Who knew?

Your body did things
I never imagined,
It was so good it brought tears to my eyes, instantly.
Hours of loving for us, thankfully
You fed me a cure for my ailment.

Who knew? Who knew?

My radar was strong, but I kept my distance.
Someone said to take one for the team and I said no…
I didn't want to be turned into a zombie,
I didn't want to crave you all the time

I tried to keep my distance until..
Well that's another story

I have the ability to see ahead and I knew
I knew.
And still…
could not change the outcome,
Damn it, I knew!

TOO MUCH

It became too much…
Yet I still pressed my luck.
I was in a daze,
Caught up in your haze.
You blew smoke and I inhaled it…
I was like an addict.
Too much!

I craved you all the time.
Your smell the sound of your voice
The chocolate darkness of your skin had me hungry.
I wanted to run my fingers through your silky hair,
The way your eyes slanted at the corners had me in a trance.
Your smile was infectious.
Too much!

My heart swelled and I was in love,
I didn't even know when it happened.
The affection you showed me surprised me,
I yearned for it ran to it.
Too much!

All I needed was some good love,
Honesty, and loyalty.
Didn't I deserve it.
I changed my world for you,
I would have stopped it for you.
Too much!

MY SECRET HELL

Loved you too strongly too passionately,
Gave it all without abandon without thought.
I mourn your touch and your kiss,
Left to die in a passionless Hell.
I have the memories, the thoughts,
I wake up every day trying to give it all I got.

I wail, I moan, but I don't drop it like it hot,
I'm in an erotic purgatory.
Stuck lonely in Hell, but it's safer that way,
I placed that side of me behind bars.

I wake in the middle of the night with a gasp,
Nope it wasn't a dream it's still there.
The pain the emptiness you left in place,
Yep, its pure Hell.

Will it ever just go?
I need it to…
The pain,
Just… Can't… Stay!

YOUR TONGUE

Your tongue made me think, sit, and contemplate it.
It's touched me everywhere.
Head to toe,
Wet slide made me glow,
I pushed to get you to my sweet spot.

The sucks and licks bent me to your will,
The air caught your name and
Tucked it away in secret.
Your tongue was but magical.

It could love and it could punish,
I tried to be a good girl even though my bad side deserved a slip and slide.

Slip and slide was what we created.
We slid our way to ecstasy often,
I cried out and you appreciated the sound and rewarded me.
Say my name Boo!

Your tongue touched me from,
Head to toe and back again.
Wet ride wet night.
I begged for it,
You loved it!

OWN IT

I feel my hips rock from side to side as I walk in
I know your eyes follow.
I smile I love to tease,
I move my body to the beat.
I feel the air kiss my skin as I take off my shirt.
My breast peek-a-boo over the black lace
Marinate in it baby…
I own it!

My skirt follows,
I melt from the way you look at me.
The lace of my panties glide across my skin
I get wetter as you lick your lips.
I can be whatever flavor you crave,
I own it!

I laugh as you grab me,
I know your control was close,
To the breaking point.
I bend in front of you so my softness,
Can touch you where you are hard?
Thank you, baby… for letting me feel it.
I slide against you to tease your mind,
I own it!

Sex, Love, & Romance

We dance to our own special beat.
We love hard and deep.
Turning night into the morning
Thank You baby I breathe at the end.
I own it!

I LOVE

I love when you wake me and take me.
I love that smile.
I love the feathery way you touch me.
I enjoy the love we make.

I love how you say my name.
I love the way you tease me.
I love it when you please me.
I love the way you make me quake.

I love that shit, put this on a plate and sop it up.
I love the bounce and the roll we create.
I love the sounds we make.
I love that oohs and that ahhs.
Baby, keep it up!

I love that hip flow and when you dip low.
Keep me cumin'
I love it!

YOU'VE GOT ME

The only thing between us is our skin,
Sweat coats us,
We make love all night,
You've got me.

Our lips touch,
Our eyes meet,
Our limbs intertwined,
You've got me.

You rub my heated skin and I melt more,
You kiss it to cool it and we both go up,
We erupt together in a liquid flame,
You've got me.

Jeff Ellis & LaKeah Shannelle

THE FIRST TIME

The first time was an accident.
We were trying to keep warm in the frigid fall air.
Our heads turned at the same time and our lips met.
We moved in slow motion as time stood still.

You walked me inside and turned me around.
Your hands wrapped around my waist.
I surrendered to your will,
I was shocked by how energized you made me feel.
For once I didn't have to be in control
I could just enjoy.

Our clothes melted away as we slowly kissed.
We took our time to learn each-other.
I laid back and closed my eyes for this ride,
You didn't disappoint me as I cried out.
Time after time,
You were my friend this was not part of the plan.

For a decade you have not stopped surprising me
Happy ten years since that surprising night
You blew my mind and that continued.

OUR HIDEAWAY

The walk was not far the hideaway was in reach.
We looked here and there to make sure there was no breach.
No one else was allowed, to our little place.
You laid me out and worshipped me on our altar of love.

The hideaway was our secret spot.
You often bent me over and took me up top.
Out there with nature, we could be naked and free.
We didn't worry about who could see us,
We wanted to just be.

Our ecstasy was spread all over our rock.
The inhabitants of the area witnessed our love.
You whisper your feelings like I couldn't hear.
I pretend I didn't, to keep you near.

Our hideaway wasn't just a physical spot.
It was hidden in you,
Because you hold the key.

To what we chose to be.
To our elevation and growth,

Jeff Ellis & LaKeah Shannelle

As long as you keep it hidden.

Our love will be no non-existent
And continue to be hidden away.

Sex, Love, & Romance

MORE

I want your head in my lap,
As I rub your head,
Feeling happiness and trust,
As you give me more.
I have no problems,
Giving you my all.

It was you it was easy,
I'll give you more,
Give as much as I do,
I need your loyalty Boo.

We think so differently,
The more I want to give,
I feel like you want to leave,
I try not to push or nag.
My love is all I had to give,
I just want to give you more.

Is my love stifling or too much?

I promise you I just want to touch,
Touch your heart and mind,
I gave you so much of my time.

I'll give you more, but you have to go first.

You have to show me that,
I'm enough,

Jeff Ellis & LaKeah Shannelle

I can't make this work on my own.
You have to make me feel like I belong.

The sad thing is,
I would give you more but…
I have no more to give.

I SEE YOU

I see you,
I'm scared to fall again.
I don't want to be hurt, I can't take it,
But I see you.

I hear you breath,
I can smell your heat,
I can taste your sweetness,
I want to touch your skin,
I see you.

Please don't hurt me,
I'm just in a quest for your manliness,
Come close,
Come kiss me,
Let me see you.

I need you to know I already do,
You can't hide.

I see you…
I do!

I hide it, it's safer,
I feel like I'm in hiding,
I cry in private,
I miss you,
But I see you.

Sex, Love, & Romance

WANT

I fell deep,
Did I fall alone,
All I want is for you to love me.

Do you love me?
Is this a game to you?
Questions, questions stop asking the questions.

Is this love? What do you want?
You said you weren't ready,
You weren't ready for me,
But you were ready for another.

If you love me, then why?
Why?
Say so…

I have no answers,
Will I ever?

I ask the wind,
It whispers your name.

I want to know,
I want all of you,
I will not accept any less.

I want a whole heart,
Stop breaking it,

Jeff Ellis & LaKeah Shannelle

The pain is too much.

Fix It

I want completion,
Was I too old?
Was I too big?
Was I not the right color?
Was I just not enough?

What do you want?

Jeff Ellis & LaKeah Shannelle

PLAYTIME

I want to play,
I want to be light and flirtatious,
I think I forgot,
Can I play with you?
I want to remember how.

I want to frolic in the sun and,
Play in the waves of the sea,
Will you join me?
Put aside everything come with me,
Life needs a break I need you.

Remember how to laugh and flirt?
Steal secret kisses in the corner?
Can we make love in the sun?

You feel so good,
Not just your body but your love.
Make me laugh again,
Let's run in the flow of the sand.

Take my hand,
Trust me I will not lead you astray.
Follow me,
Our love will lead the way.

We missed out on so much,
We never got the opportunity.
Come on let's get way,

Lead the way.

SCHOOL OF HARD KNOCKS

Why didn't you teach me how to love you?
I tried to love you like you've never been before,
I gave you my heart, mind, body, and soul freely.
All you had to do was teach me.

You have shared with me things.

You never tell,
Or so you say,
You shared the hurts,
You shared your dreams,
You shared your gifts,
Please just show me what I need to do.

Maybe I failed at being the teacher,
I thought I was showing you how,
I wanted our love to be unconditional,
Free, didn't mean go with another.

I think I failed and the student,
Became the teacher.

Jeff Ellis & LaKeah Shannelle

Now I'm changed I learned a hard lesson.

This student of life has grown,
Into something different.

A MAN'S GAME

We can have fun you can be mine for a moment,
You're free to do what you want and so am I,
I don't want the pressure to stay and please,
Let's just have fun.

Your time when I need it,
Your lips when I need it,
Me and you when... I... need... it!
It's about what I need.

But wait…
You please me and you will be pleased as well,
It's my gig I'm in control,
Maybe tomorrow I'll want Sam or Tom,
Don't worry I'm just playing a man's game.

It's called my way,
Let's pretend for a couple nights,
That you are mine,
Then I'll release you.

Wink, wink. don't worry I'll let you go,
Don't want you to get bored.

Listen up…
You'll like it because I love it,
It sounds good to me,
What do you say?

MY PLAYLIST OF EMOTIONS

How many times have I said I'm through?
Yet here I am,
When did it happen?
Was I blindsided?
How did I get here?

Where can I turn when I need love?
Where can I go?
I don't want to be your little secret,
I'm better than that!

You've got me gone,
Monica said it better, but I continued it,
So unreal.

Your rain gently touched my soul,
It cooled the fire,
And I lost control,
My passion was about to explode.

I was caught in your storm and I never knew I needed shelter,
Until you rained down on me.

Sex, Love, & Romance

I look in the mirror at the pieces of this woman left behind,
And I feel down and out,
This is not what love is supposed to be about,
Over and over, I try and over and over I cry.
Oh, rain on me.

As I stand in the rain, I hear.
Long as I live, I'll never get over,
If I can't be with the one, I love I'll just do the two-step with the one I'm with.
It's killing me, but it's okay.

I adjust the volume as my soul heals,
I know I'll always be his lady,
His soul is calling out my name.

They say if you love something you've got to let it go,
And if it comes back then it means so much more.

But if it never does at least you will know,
That it was something you had to go through to grow.

My strength grew as I listened to my playlist,
In my heart in my mind
I am ready for love.

Jeff Ellis & LaKeah Shannelle

STANDING STILL

I am on the ocean with movement and yet I feel like I am standing still.
I feel like the world has passed me by,
I feel left behind.
In the ocean without a life raft
Somebody rescue me.

Wrap me in your arms and give me life,
Kiss me with the breath of life,
Rub me to warm me,
Awaken my passion,
Light my fire.

Share your life,
We can live better,
We can complete a breath together,
Let's be as one.

The ocean won't keep me still,
Let's fly to the cosmos and count the stars,
Zip back in time and find our ancestors,
Let's see if we were meant to be one,
They will let us know.

I want to be in complete Zen,
I need peace,
I don't want to keep being star crossed,
I need to be together and loved wholly,
Without the sun, moon, and stars getting in the way.

Sex, Love, & Romance

AMAZING LOVE

One day I will sing to you about how amazing your love was,
It touched my heart and filled it with strength.
I floated on cloud nine,
All that was missing was the ring.

You burned my soul with how deeply you looked into my eyes,
You allowed me to know what you carried deep,
It never faltered I wanted to keep that feeling.
You captured me

I don't know how we thought we were only going to be friends,
You sizzled my body just by standing close.
You made any excuse to touch me,
Uness we were alone, then you stayed far away,
I thought you couldn't be approached.

I was there during some of your hard times,
As you were for mines.
A Christmas and dinner was the sweetest,
That Snickers on Valentines was the best,
The birthday loving was memorable.

Your smile and laugh always topped my day,
Thank you for being there,
It was not perfect but I know it was real.

JUST ONE TIME

Let me love you just one time.
No one has to know.
It's just for us.
Your soul is screaming my name.

I don't know what you are missing.
Let me know and I'll give it,
I can turn into a Vixen,
Give you your desire,

Tell me it will be our secret,
Play the role just one time,
I can feel your vibe,
You need one night,

I hope I'm not begging,
You probably have a line waiting.
Every kind of girl to do your bidding.

If that night won't happen,
It's okay I'll forget this conversation.
Tuck it in my secret place and,
I'll leave it there.

ROMANTIC LOVE

Who would have thought my hood man was secretly a romantic?
Poems he writes lyrics he lets flow…
He tells his feelings and puts on a show,
He gave me a million kisses and
He never wanted to stop.
I didn't want him to…
It would never be enough.

The loving way you set up the living room,
For the sexy deep loving, you gave me,
The way you knew my favorite things and made sure I had them,
To the way you bathed me in the tub.

You rubbed me down and oiled my skin lovingly,
It blew me away, but I kept your secret,
No one else knew.

You had me aww struck,
None had loved me so thoroughly,

Jeff Ellis & LaKeah Shannelle

Thank you for setting the bar so high.

There will never be another to quench,
My insatiable thirst,
With a sweet and loving romantic flare,
And then toss in the thug to my sexual mug.
To even out the flavor…

You created a new drink for my never-ending need,
I drank from the chalice often.

Rhythm and Blues

You rocked to my roll I danced to your beat,
I didn't think it would work.
Didn't think we were in sync,
I hipped to your hop you gave the rhythm,
To my Blues.

I thought our beat wouldn't,
Match up,
But our allegro had us popping.

I was in major you were in minor,
Somewhere in the middle we found sweet harmony.

Our Symphony created a love song so sweet,
That we were careful to never miss a beat.
We rocked and rolled all night long,
Until the perfect Jazz notes scaled the walls.

We created a perfect harmony.

We were more than just a melody so much more,
Than a rhyme we had found a love that would transcend time.

Jeff Ellis & LaKeah Shannelle

Jeff's Thoughts

COLORS

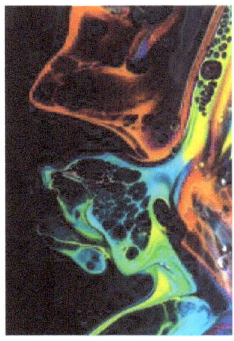

I can see more colors of the rainbow and
It is because of you.
I admire your head to the wind attitude with all you've been through.
I can't hide the love that I have for you,
Even with time our love is still on fire and blazing.

I have never met anyone like you,
To me your personality is amazing.
We team up in life and stick together,
Like worker bees.
You inspire me to be my best and
To never give you less of me.
Until I met you in the area of love,
I felt cursed.

No matter what I did in previous situations,
Things only got worse.
It's different with you,

Jeff Ellis & LaKeah Shannelle

No matter my request,
You quench my thirst.

In all the decades I have roamed
This planet that's a first.
I think about your tenderness,
Your deep love that's so true.
Every time I visualize it,
I smile and fall more in love with you.

WELL HERE NOW

Sometimes progress looks like no sleep,
In this world of complexity, you have to alternate,
Between the lion and the sheep.

Bleep this world,
Pull your bootstraps up from your feet.
Run head-on at failure or defeat,
You could never win if you don't compete.

I say all that to say,
My time is short and I'm always late.
I always feel like I've got to push the bar,
Because I can't wait.

However long you live that ain't a long time.
No matter how far you climb,
It's never too late to be in your prime.

Someone once told me that I would lose everything in life,
For how I work and sacrifice.
I told them that means,
I will only come back twice as nice.

For what you thought I was sacrificing,
I was acquiring the skills to get more.
My fearlessness to explore.
It will yield me better than before.

POUND TOWN

All aboard, express ride to pound town,
With a long ride like an amusement park
With ups and downs.

Meet me at the gate and we going to
The kissing booth
Imma put my tongue in your mouth,
Unbutton your shirt… get loose.

Now that your mouth is wet,
I'm sending you south,
To polish the hood of my corvette

Next booth we are filling your mouth,
With my water gun.
To release all my milky pressure,
I feel a ton.

You are taking your time on this ride to pound town,
It's all fun going down.
On you like ice cream dripping off your cones.
Your smile and glasses excite me to my bones.

Years later we still at pound town and we have,
Never thought about finding our way home.

Sex, Love, & Romance

Your whispers set my ears on fire,
Licking both lips covers my desires, I ain't never alone.

VOICES

Grateful and blessed for the provider,
Of all living things.
Giving hope and compassion,
Every single second of the day.

You can feel the love touching,
You 93 million miles away.
One of the purest forms of love spreading,
Light in the darkest of times.

Priming my soul to motivate and grind,
Any height I need to reach,
I know that I can climb.

When I'm not doing my best your
Love and warmth inspire me.
When I'm in the zone my sun connects
With you and set fire to me.

Your love gives me the same blazing shivers,
With feelings that rush and
Flow as deep as rivers
I can be as far as the earth is,
Away from the sun.

But no matter how far away
We are from each other.
I know we are still one.

PASSING THOUGHTS

I'm looking for you baby where are you at,
You been on my mind daily and,
I need you in my life.
I'm looking for my soulmate to make my wife.
To love her till my last days and to treat her right,
She is the light of my life, scorching through it bright.

Flying me to lands of love and compassion,
I'll admit when I first met you it was all about smashin.

Having fun or a night out then drilling and bashing,
The better I got to know you my notions,
Oh, I started rehashing.
Is it possible that I could be working on something soon to be classic?

Our time together is incredible and so much fun,
We move in harmony and our hearts beat as one.

Your outside beauty is only a portion of
What's inside.
When I'm inside I feel the powerful momentum of the tide.

TIC TOC

Breath so sweet, lips so soft,
Skin is timeless, to have missed her is your loss.
The love comes in waves filling your,
Minutes, hours, and days.

Your love is brighter than the stars rays,
With a beauty that surpasses descriptions.
To any ailment, I might have you smile as my prescription.

Some people have never seen perfection in physical,
Form and perceive this as fiction.
I feel in everyone's lifetime that they get
At least one chance.

One chance to take advantage of love in this,
Universe and advance.
To hold hands, share essence, and birth romance,
Spooning and going for long walks
Eating slow because I enjoy the intriguing talks.

LICKING MY LIPS

You make me feel like nobody,
Has ever made me feel.
Your sex appeal is serious and gives me chills.

Put you on my plate and feast,
For an everlasting meal.
To be without you is something,
I never wanna feel.

Even the thought is disruptive,
And makes my heart sink.
As sure as I breathe air and,
As sure as I pen this ink.
For the gates of love and happiness
You are my link.

When I'm sexual with you, your love,
Brings out my freak.
When we don't exchange bodily fluids and
Argue I feel weak.

When you're not in my arms
I can't smell your hair or sleep.
I got to get inside you, I got to give it to you deep.

Jeff Ellis & LaKeah Shannelle

It's hard to even finish this because,
I'm thinking about you each and every line.
How tasty your lips feel, and how good you can grind.

How I keep falling in love with you time after time.

WITH EVERY PASSING BREATHS

I did my best to hold back the tears,
I thought about the dedication I had gained throughout the years.
Remembering all the special moments,
We shared in time.

Because of my love for you regularly,
You cross my mind.
Wondering are you reaching for,
Me like I'm reaching for you,
I would like to think so and would love if you dropped me a clue.

Open up the skies and pour out the rain,
I'm missing you I haven't found anything,
To sooth the pain
I keep myself busy with work to help me maintain.

If I wasn't doing that, I would be sitting,
Around idle going insane.

Look for what happen, why you not with
Me and who's the blame,
Instead I revel in my love campaign,
Living off the old love to sustain.

SHADOW HOURS

As the night falls all my thoughts are on you
As I look at the moon, I can't help but
To think about us.

The kissing the touching the love the lust,
I think about toiling through the night,
Leaving you alone
I'm contemplating wrapping my arms,
Around you when I get home.

You fit perfectly in my arms each and every time,
The chemistry we make when we make love,
Is devine.

Your loving passion gets all of my attention and
A full erection.
I look forward daily to your
Conversations and affection.

You helped me to learn to love myself,
With all my imperfections

Sex, Love, & Romance

We are soulmates I love our interconnection.

Or how you finish what I'm about to say,
You make me feel like a child again and
I wanna play.

I'M COUNTING

How many ways can I say I love you?
Flowers are cool and dinner is nice,
How do you thank the woman who
changed your life?

Curves we done had and valleys we done walked through.
I still feel good to look you in the eye and say I Love you when
I talk to you.

Many times you have shown me a point of view
I would have never saw.
Win, loose, or draw with you on my team
I'm sure to correct my flaws.

My appreciation for you will forever run deep,
I knew you was the one and already gave you,
My heart to keep.

I wanna thank you for your
Dedication and time served.
You revamped my life and
Kept our love preserved.

Buying you something is nice but a
Hug and kiss, is more revealing.
You can touch me, look in my eyes, and catch all These
thoughts and feelings.

INTERSTELLAR

I breathe to your heartbeat and
Walk to your breath.
We will still be together far beyond death,
The love I have for you can't be contained,
In one body or vessel.

I'm trying to tell you my love will be with you far after my body has departed and left you,
Yet closer than the skin you're in for sure.

As my love travel throughout the multiverse
My love for you grows.
Like the plants in my window in the
Wintertime we thrive.

You have me feeling like all I need is,
Your love to survive.
My gratitude is eternal for helping me,
Reach phenomenal heights.

You have taken me to places I couldn't,
See with my own eyes.
In the darkest hour in this sea of life I look to you as my beacon of light.

Shine your light on me and by all,
Means open your life giver.

Jeff Ellis & LaKeah Shannelle

Every drop of love that's in me,
I'm ready to deliver.

COMPLETION

If I have not told you, you help make,
My life complete
Sit down take a load off, let me tend to
You and rub your feet.

Massaging your feet and ankles does
Something to me, it kind of puts me at peace,
As my hands move up and down your legs, I can Feel some of your tension starting to release.

As I look up into the most beautiful
Eyes to hear you speak,
Listening to your words spew from
Your soft cheeks.

Telling me thank you for massaging,
Your feet and legs
Oh, that's no problem we might as well do the Rest if you got time, I'll go ahead.

I scan your anatomic composition,
As if I have infrared,
I'll move to your shoulders then work,
Up to your neck.

All along whispering how I feel about,
You with a kissing effect
I can feel the warmth and comfort from the energy you project.

Our conversation is so sensual as I run my Fingers through your hair,
I know the sparks between us eventual,
Will start a flare.

And then boom our lips lock and I knew what I thought was ever so true.
The person I kept dreaming about spending the rest of my life with was you.

SAY LESS

Unbelievable you taste better than the
Gas that I blow.

Luscious lips shapely hips ready to
Put on a show.

I can see your vibrating even,
At a glance.

I try not to stare as you move through,
Your transient dance.

Your eyes are very deep and pierces,
My heart like a lance.

Every part of your body moves together,
With perfect timing.

With ass and titties shimmying
Your body moves as if it's rhyming.

As you move closer to me the effects get stronger
I can feel it happening my,
Erection getting longer.

I'm getting over excited looking for,
The place to plug in.

I'm in pre-ejaculation, thickness go on and

Jeff Ellis & LaKeah Shannelle

Let a thug in.

Chill out and relax, take advantage of tonight,
While I stretch out your back with
Endless hours of chocolate pipage.

THE SET UP

Excuse me, do you wear chokers because you like getting choked?
You look like you could take all this chocolate Down your throat.

You look like the type that would come out Naked only dressed in a coat.
You put the sexy back in woman and give,
Me and my manhood hope.

Your eyes are telling me to take them pretty Panties off and have a piece.
If the buffet looks as good as the appetizer, then imma have a feast.

Kiss her, lick her, until she moans,
Deeply and release
To bathe in her juicy preliminary for
The next round.

She has just left earth and landed in pound town,
Her lips wrapped around my,
Massive organ pulsating.

My breath is getting heavier while she goes,
Up and down and I'm anticipating,
My heart beating, my legs shaking and then, she Puts me to sleep.

SLOW ROUNDS

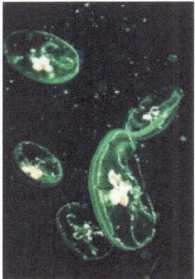

I can't recount because it's been ever too long,
Since the last time my tongue has slipped between your thong?

To navigate and open the doors of juicy juice,
To feel your hips, relax, then tense up,
Then get loose.

Tasting your chemistry of love until a
Climax is induced,
That's just part one of part deuce,
In segment two is when my chocolate bar
Gets introduced.

Like a serpent I'm mesmerized by the
Movement of your waist
It's composed of the finest regions,
I'll have a taste.

Rise and descend slowly baby no need for haste,
When I explode, I need you to clean up all traces,
Sometimes I think we rush through our work, but I like to take my time.
Knowing how things are here today gone tomorrow I like to savor mines.

ADDICTED

Its damn funny what love can make,
You want to do.
You always on my mind even when
I don't I think of you.

Even if I went blind and never saw you again,
I could never forget you or get you out my mind.
I knew when I met you the feelings I felt,
That it was a sign.

But it's hard sometimes to sit down and
Open my feeling to express,
I been closed up like a box most of my life.
Even with love pushing me it's hard,
To get it off my chest.

But your inspiration is a turn on to
The highest degree
Your soft kisses on my neck and
Your even softer voice is…
A dick hardening guarantee,
I'm addicted to you and this is something,
That I know
I don't know if it's how you make my mind grow,
Or if it's how you make my organs blow

When I'm around you and when I'm not around It's not hard to tell I know it show.
You are part of my heart, soul, and peace,
Of the many things you can claim you are the,
Tamer of the savage beast…

There is no fighting your pheromone touch,

Jeff Ellis & LaKeah Shannelle

Since you have been in my presence.
I have been in your clutch,
I don't know if it's the overstanding you bring As to why I love you so much.

Through our experiences, orgasms, and time,
I Look at love a whole different way,
I know I don't deserve you in this lifetime,
So, I secretly work at being a better me everyday.
When I think about us throughout the years,
I Hold back the tears because I know you grew me,
For that I'm ever grateful truly.

HOLDING YOU

I just want to hold you,
To wrap my arms around you
Tighter than your skin.

Its like sparks start with the smiles and grins,
That opens up the enlightening conversation,
I'm pulled into your eyes as if they
Were tracker beams.

The sparkle, the shimmer, oh, how
Your eyes gleam,
Love, truth, and warmth pours from your eyes,
I love telling you about my day,
The lows, and the highs.

I can feel your understanding for
All my attempts to explain,
My experiences in growth, love, loss, and pain
At every turn I can feel your
Compassion and concern.

I been cool for a while but since you been gone,
To see you my heart yearns.
Only to tell you I love and appreciate all the time,
You have taught me true love and it's forever,
Embedded in my mind.

Jeff Ellis & LaKeah Shannelle

BINARY STAR

From two different universes but I feel like
We were meant to be.
You came into my life like a gust of wind that blew away the debris.

The time we spend together is all out captivating,
The worlds you bring me to have,
My heart accelerating.
From your vibes like the sun,
I shine you're my moon reflecting my lighting
When we combine.

Creating a big bang that shakes our spirits,
Lighten our masses leaving us lifted.
All my energies deposited into your black hole,
Until my soul gets shifted.

Creating baby planets in deep space,
Caught in your gravitational pull.
And so there's no drifting,
I can only see life getting better through my futuristic lens.

Together we charged up like solar winds.

THE NOTES OF LOVE

When I hear it, I can feel my mind switch,
I know I'm moved by certain tones and pitch,
I know deep down inside I was a born musician,
I bathe in the tones and frequencies from above.

I can feel the sound waves opening,
My heart up to love
As the tones penetrate my body, I am relaxed,
Music can move emotions from
Minimum to max.

Sometimes I feel good sometimes I wanna cry,
Certain tones bring back memories and
I don't know why.

So, now you know I hear you like an
Orchestra, and you make my heart fly,
I'll love your music until the day I die.

Jeff Ellis & LaKeah Shannelle

DROP DROP

The warmth I feel from you brings,
Out my inner force
My thoughts of you be like mental intercourse.

Every experience blazing like a torch,
Your attractiveness amplifies my manhood,
Your company and conversation are always good.

I'm hanging onto every word as
If they were hypnotic.
Looking at your lips the fullness is erotic,
Tell me what you have done to,
Become the way you are.

I always feel comfortable around you and
My defenses drops because
The fountain of youth in your honey pot.

The explosions start inside me long,
Before we make contact
So, by the time I hit your g-spot we both climax?

ON TEN

No matter how bad I'm doing when I see you,
I know everything going to be alright,
You've opened doors in my world,
that were closed tight.

Like a magician you make opportunities appear.
That were never there.
Through your unwavering love you can,
Move a mountain I swear.

You got me hooked on your love,
Honey, like a bear
The feeling is so rare like precious,
Gems and stones.

It's nothing amateurish about this,
You're full grown,
Your love sends me off like a
Rocketship in overload.

I love walking down our yellow brick,
Road as it unfolds,
Our togetherness heats us through,
This cold world.

Shining rays of love warming cold hearts

Jeff Ellis & LaKeah Shannelle

We will exceed any boundaries or
Top any charts.

ALL IN MY MIND

Breath of fresh air
Oh, girl Love your hair.
You're a different Kool-Aid,
You really take me there.
I just love chilling with you cause,
Our times to be so nice.

However much it cost to pay attention
I'll pay the price,
The way you move,
Gracefully and so precise.
You enter like you on a
Runway about to take flight.

Your mind unfolds like wings, oh so nice,
Our unison is one of the
Livest in the flesh
Until our death we will
Move in one unified breath.

Collectively I'm respecting you and
Your respecting me
We play together in harmony, effectively,
Opposites of the same body, so we are one.

Our compliments each other
Shine bright as the sun,
We need nothing more we know,
That we are all that we need.
This has been signed sealed by a
Kiss which is our creed.

LOW FREQUENCY

This relationship is up and down like a yo-yo,
One moment I'm cool the next I'm like hell naw I can't go.

With this back and forth shit you
Never really know,
Sometimes it's all smiles but it's really just slow
Words of fire, words of hurt.

Door being slammed signs of desertion,
Feeling like I been doused with ice cold water,
These negative emotions I try not to be bothered.
Sometimes dealing with these situations
I feel emaciated and slaughtered.

I turn to empty pages to fill my soul with peace,
This is the safest playground where my
Emotions can be released.
Where nobody will get hurt and where I can
Still put in some work.

I have to get somewhere where I can release the beast.

Sex, Love, & Romance

BUTTERFLY

You used to be my tic and I was your toc,
We used to be inseparable and then something stopped.

Did we stop sharing?
Did we stop caring?

Is it because we spend less time away from each other with less hugs?
Less conversation and less love?
We don't occupy each other's day,
Like we used to.

What happened to that electrifying feeling?
I used to feel around you,
I stay throwing up the tent for
The three-ring circus.

All my attempts for reconnection seem worthless,
I used to thrive on our universal vibe.
The thoughts of you had me,
Feeling excited and alive.

To think of some of the same thoughts
Now only make me cry.
After my experience anything less
Makes me feel deprived.

I know it's about my perspective and it's all in my mind, never give up and continue to try
Until that very moment we lock eyes.

I know change is constant and painfully realize …we not the same no more.

Jeff Ellis & LaKeah Shannelle

About the Authors

LaKeah Shannelle is a multi-genre author from Cincinnati, Ohio. She discovered her love of the written word early in life. Always with a book in hand she decided why not touch the hearts of others as hers has been. A lover of people and the human emotion, she will keep you engrossed with every word no matter what genre she takes on. Take the challenge and go on the adventure with her.

She has written several stories in multiple anthologies. Lady's Story was her feature poetry book from her heart, and The Revenant Series is a thriller born from an intense dream that will keep you on the run. Enjoy some suspense with a side of brown sugar.

Jeff Ellis is a newly discovered author from Cincinnati Ohio. He is the devoted father of nine. He follows the traditional teachings of his ancestors and pushes himself to evolve to become the enlightened being he was created to be.

Jeff writes floetic poetry and stories that speak of Urban life and the truths of it. He wants to share his love of that life with the world, and he looks forward to connecting with readers from all over.

Jeff is living his artist dreams as he writes, paints, and creates multiple ways to express who he is to all.

Lightning Source UK Ltd.
Milton Keynes UK
UKHW051427160223
416961UK00009BA/156